Richard Caldwell

A true history of the acquisition of Washington's

headquarters at Newburgh, by the state of New York

Vol. 1

Richard Caldwell

A true history of the acquisition of Washington's headquarters at Newburgh, by the state of New York
Vol. 1

ISBN/EAN: 9783337713218

Printed in Europe, USA, Canada, Australia, Japan

Cover: Foto ©ninafisch / pixelio.de

More available books at **www.hansebooks.com**

OF

THE ACQUISITION

OF

WASHINGTON'S HEADQUARTERS

AT NEWBURGH.

By the State of New York.

BY RICHARD CALDWELL,

SALISBURY MILLS, N. Y.

STIVERS, SLAUSON & BOYD,
MIDDLETOWN, N. Y.
1887.

Miss Dr. Julia E. Bradner, President of the Old Ladies'
Society of Orange County, New York:

I have written a TRUE account of how that (which in the
past, and is in the present, as it will ever be in the future)
well-known and historic spot, Washington's Headquarters,
located at Newburgh, in this county, came to pass from
private ownership into the possession of the State of New
York.

This account has been copyrighted and will first appear in
the Middletown Daily Press, as well as in the semi-weekly
edition—The Orange County Press. It will also be printed
in Pamphlet form. The latter are to be sold. In casting
about for a local county object as a beneficiary for the resultant pecuniary benefits (if any) from the sale of these
pamphlets, I don't know of any which commends itself more
to my sympathies, as well as to my best judgment, than does
the beneficent object you have undertaken to accomplish,
which in the articles of incorporation you state to be the
"making a comfortable home in Orange County for
aged and infirm and destitute ladies of said county,
wherein the sick and enfeebled may receive all requisite care
and attention in sickness and health, and be provided a
respectable burial at death." In the furtherance of this
truly commendable object I hereby offer you all the proceeds which there may be from the sale of these pamphlets, after deducting the cost of their publication and any
attendant expenses of such sale.

Very respectfully your well-wisher in the work you have
undertaken,   RICHARD CALDWELL.
Salisbury Mills, N. Y., January 18th, 1887.

To Mr. R. Caldwell:

Dear Sir:—In behalf of the cause which we have so
much at heart, I thank you for your kind offer of the proceeds of sale of the Headquarters article, hoping we may
realize something in aid of an object so dear to us.

Respectfully yours,
JULIA E. BRADNER,
President Orange County Home Society.
Middletown, January 20th, 1887.

INTRODUCTORY.

Mr. E. M. Ruttenber, in his history of Orange County, under the head of "Washington's Headquarters," on pages 283 and 284 says: "A large, and in some departments valuable collection of manuscripts and relics is now deposited in the building, for which, as well as for the INITIAL steps, by which the State authorities were induced to purchase the property, the public are mainly indebted to the late Enoch Carter, although many other articles of value have been added by other parties, and especially by the State and Federal authorities."

That the statement above made in respect to the collection of relics and manuscripts gathered in the building is correct, the writer believes, for Mr. Carter's large heart and public spirit and patriotic impulses were well known. That they went beyond those of his fellow townsmen at the time, in respect to his efforts to gain possession for the State, of the Headquarters property itself, the writer also knows. He further knows that while Mr. Carter was heartily in sympathy with the movement to gain such possession, "the public are (not) mainly indebted to him for the intitial steps by which the State authorities were induced to purchase the property," but to another person, as the following article will most conclusively show.

It is further believed that Mr. Ruttenber has unintentionally been led into the statement above copied from his history, a statement he would not have made if he had known all the facts.

THE HISTORY.

To the many from all parts of the world who have visited the beautiful and historic grounds at Washington's Headquarters, in Newburgh, the secret history of how they came into the possession of the State may not be known. Indeed, it is believed that very few, if any, persons in Newburgh itself know of this history, and how near this (to the country) valuable property came to passing into private hands. We are told in Holy Writ, that in one period of the world's history, or more especially in one period of the history of Egypt, "a King arose who knew not Joseph," meaning that the past benefits which that wonderful man had conferred on the Egyptian Monarchy, had, in the lapse of time, the busy onrush of the present, and more particularly in the jealousy of the rising, growing power within her midst, been forgotten, and the name of the man who pre-eminently above all others had been the means of her exaltation, was heard no more in the land as the founder of her greatness, and her saviour in the years of her dire distress. Not with the idea or intention, for a moment, of claiming that there is a parallel between Joseph, the great Governor of Egypt, with his prophetic, far-seeing and out-reaching plans which involved the destiny of two nations for all future time, and that of the foresight and out-reaching plan of the humble individual in private life, whose connection with the salvation of Washington's Headquarters is now to be given. Yet, history which records the greatness and deeds of the one on the sacred page, to be true and just, ought also to record the fact that to the exertions of ONE man Newburgh is indebted to-day for the fact that the Headquarters property belongs to the State of New York, and not to a private individual, or perhaps three individuals.

To give the history: As is well known, the property in Revolutionary times, and before, and after, was known as "The Hasbrouck Property;" the house as "The Old Hasbrouck House," and so named in public papers of that day. For how long it was in the possession of the Hasbrouck family anterior to the time when it became the property of Jonathan Hasbrouck (the last of the name who owned it) is to the writer unknown. But it must have been for a considerable period, from the fact that it had come to be identified with the family name, and also that it was cherished as a most precious heir-loom by the members of the family, and by Jonathan especially, the last owner of the name, whose heart strings were torn when it was forever alienated from him. To extricate himself from the financial difficulties which in the latter years of his life seemed like a spider's web to environ the old man in their meshes, Jonathan Hasbrouck and Phebe, his wife, mortgaged "The Hasbrouck Property" to the "Commissioners of the United States Deposit Fund" for the County of Orange, on the 12th day of July, in the year 1837, for $2,000. For many years the annual interest was regularly paid in the month of October, the time prescribed by law. "But it fell on a day" (the first Tuesday of October, 1848) that the old man could not make his annual payment, on the last day of the four, in that month, on which he had the option of paying, nor could he at the end of the week of grace thereafter, which the law gave, nor at the end of the three months advertised time of sale under foreclosure. It was truly pitiful the efforts which the old man made to save his heart-treasured possession, which had for so long a time been in his family, and it would almost bring tears to the eyes of Mr. Caldwell, one of the Commissioners, the letters he received during these three months from Jonathan Hasbrouck to know if there could not be some further delay in the proceedings, to give him a chance to raise the amount due on the mortgage, a chance which the old man always saw a little way ahead. But the "Book of Instructions," for the Commissioners' guidance as to their duties, was very plain and explicit, and any deviation to the detriment of the fund would have incurred to themselves personal liability, as well as malfeasance. If the writer remembers correctly, the two Commissioners told Mr. Hasbrouck that if he could raise the money within the time limit of the law, they would remit all fees and commissions which the law allowed them. But he could not.

SALE OF THE PROPERTY.

It was put up for sale, and no person appearing to bid the amount due, it was bid in by the Commissioners for and on account of the United States Deposit Fund, at the Court House, in Goshen, on the first Tuesday in February, 1849. The old man was at the sale, and when it was finally struck off he burst into tears.

The law provides that Appraisers shall be appointed by the Commissioners who shall put a value on the property, when it is, after a prescribed time, to be again offered for sale; if no bid is received equal to the appraised value, the Commissioners are to bid that sum, and the property becomes the State's absolutely. This they did. It should be said, however, that the mortgagor had the right to redeem the property at the appraised value and costs of sale. Old

10

Mr. Hasbrouck in the interim was trying to raise the money to pay off the claims, but never succeeded. The Commissioners, who were Andrew J. Caldwell, of Blooming Grove, and Alexander Campbell, of Monroe, were made custodians of the property after the sale, by the then Comptroller of the State, Hon. Washington Hunt, and it was by them put in charge of a keeper. It was at this time that efforts were made by private parties, both by letters and through personal interview with the Commis-

ANDREW J. CALDWELL.
[Taken when 80 years of age.]

sioners or rather Commissioner (for Mr. Caldwell was, by the acquiescence of "Father Campbell," the prominent man in the transaction) to induce him to use his influence with the Comptroller to sell the property to them, which he would have done if the Commissioners had so advised, and the recollection is (which, however, may not be correct) that a less sum was offered than the amount of appraisal and interest to time of the offer. Mr. Caldwell declined, as he had other plans and purposes.

ALEXANDER CAMPBELL.
[From a likeness taken in 1852.]

EFFORTS TO INDUCE RESIDENTS OF NEWBURGH TO BUY THE PROPERTY.

First he tried to induce private parties in Newburgh to
subscribe a sum sufficient to liquidate the Deposit Fund
claim. In this effort he was heartily seconded by the late
Enoch Carter, Esq., who, as far as his desires and pecuniary
ability went, was as public-spirited a man as Newburgh ever
possessed. But love of money was greater among the men of
means of Newburgh at the time, than love of patriotism, or at
least of Washington's Headquarters. Mr. Carter was much
disappointed and out of patience at the action, or rather
non-action, of his fellow townsmen, and gave expression to
his opinion of them in words which those who remember him
well can very well imagine were much more emphatic than
Scriptual.

PLANS PROPOSED.

Then Mr. Caldwell entered into correspondence with Hon.
Hamilton Fish, the then Governor of the State, proposing
two plans. One was for the Legislature of New York to
memorialize Congress to remit its claim on the State of
New York for the amount due the United States Deposit
Fund to a sum equal to the amount of the mortgage, $2,000,
with accrued interest and expenses. This is the plan which
Mr. Caldwell favored, as in case they did, it would not
cost the State any money. The other plan was for the Legislature to appropriate a sum sufficient to discharge all the
amount due to the Fund, the law requiring that the principal
of the Fund should always be kept intact.

THE GOVERNOR'S WISDOM.

The Governor chose the latter course as being more direct
and expeditious, and in this he undoubtedly showed his

12   WASHINGTON'S HEADQUARTERS.

wisdom, for if application had been made to Congress, action would perhaps have been delayed through opposition of interested parties who had their own private schemes and purposes to carry out. Governor Fish in his first annual message, after his attention had been called to the subject, asked or recommended that the Legislature appropriate the sum required, which they did, and so the property became the State's, absolutely and forever. The Deposit Fund was fully reimbursed, and private parties who wanted to make a big speculation out of the old historic spot were foiled in their purpose. The correspondence between Mr. Caldwell and Governor Fish, which was placed before the Board of Trustees by George Cornwall, Esq., once a Trustee of the Village of Newburgh, and up to his death President of the Highland Bank of that place, is here given, transcribed from the public records of the then Village of Newburgh, as well as the resolution of the Trustees of that village on the subject:

NEWBURGH, May 8, 1850.

ANDREW J. CALDWELL, ESQ.:

DEAR SIR:—It affords me great pleasure to be enabled to lay your correspondence with Gov. Fish before the Committee on Washington's Headquarters, and subsequently, before our Board of Trustees. The action of the latter body upon the subject you will find enclosed, together with the papers sent me.   I remain very respectfully yours, etc.,

GEORGE CORNWALL.

The above Committee was probably the one appointed to make arrangements for and take charge of the dedication ceremonies, July 4th, 1850.

THE CORRESPONDENCE.

At a special meeting of the Board of Trustees of the Village of Newburgh, held at the United States Hotel, on

Wednesday, April 24th, 1850, the following resolutions were unanimously adopted:

RESOLVED, That on behalf of the citizens of Newburgh, and the public generally, the thanks of this Board be tendered to Andrew J. Caldwell, Esq., Commissioner of Loans, for his early and efficient exertions to obtain the passage of the act by the Legislature to retain the title to the grounds known as Washington's Headquarters, and making them forever public grounds, and that his correspondence with Gov. Fish upon the subject be entered upon the minutes of the Board, and that a copy of this resolution be forwarded to Mr. Caldwell.

Signed, JACKSON OAKLEY,

Newburgh, May 8, 1850.   Clerk.

ANDREW J. CALDWELL TO GOV. FISH:

SALISBURY MILLS, Orange County, 1st Oct., 1849.

SIR—I beg leave to bring to your notice a transaction in which I have been concerned, in the discharge of official duty, and which I venture to presume will not be considered unworthy the Chief Magistrate of the State of New York.

The Commissioners of the United States Deposit Fund of the County of Orange, in pursuance of law, have exposed to public sale the premises in the Village of Newburgh, containing the old stone house known as "Washington's Headquarters," and have bid in the same on behalf of the State.

The place consecrated by so many interesting associations has become the property of the State, and in the ordinary course is to be sold by the Commissioners of the Land Office, for the benefit of the United States Deposit Fund. I need not remind you sir, that the old stone house was the residence of Washington's family for the last two years of the war; that there he received the news of peace, there he disbanded the Army of the Revolution, and when that army, goaded almost to desperation in view of their wrongs as set forth in the famous "Newburgh Letters," were preparing to enforce their claims at the point of the bayonet, then and there it was he achieved the crowning glory of his military career, issued his imcomparable address to the army, soothed the angry passions of the excited soldiery, averted the theatened storm, and thus ONCE MORE saved the Republic. I venture sir, to submit to you whether it would be creditable for the State of New York to sell this venerable and hallowed spot which has now come into its possession, or whether on the other hand it would not be more to the honor of the State, and in accordance with public sentiment, to hand it down to posterity as a monument to the memory of its former revered and illustrious occupant, and an enduring memorial of the interesting transactions of which it was the scene. Should the authorities of the State concur in these views, it would not be difficult to devise a plan, by which, under sanction of law, the preservation of the premises as a public ground might be effectually secured. It must be borne in mind that these premises have cost the State nothing, and if the competent authorities should see fit to transfer the charge to any public body, for public uses, there can be no doubt that the United States would release forever their interest in the Deposit Fund to that amount. In taking this liberty, I feel the greater confidence, in that the appeal is to one whose name and family are so intimately connected with the times, and transactions to which it refers.

I have the honor to be, Sir
Your most ob't servant,
ANDREW J. CALDWELL.

GOV. FISH'S REPLY:

NEW YORK, Oct. 6th, 1849.
ANDREW J. CALDWELL, ESQ.,
Salisbury Mills, Orange County.
SIR:—I am this day favored with your letter of 1st inst. (forwarded to me from Albany) referring to the sale, by the Commissioners in your County for loaning certain monies of the U. S., of the old House known as "Washington's Headquarters." I concur entirely in the views which you have

HON. HAMILTON FISH.

[Engraved by Leon Barritt, Middletown, N. Y., from a photograph taken in 1875.]

expressed of the propriety of securing this hallowed spot for some public object suitable and appropriate to its history, and I should be most happy to give any aid within the sphere of my duties, which will ensure this end. It will give me pleasure to hear from you on the subject as to any memorial which may be made by the citizens in the neighborhood. With very great regards,

Your ob't servant,

HAMILTON FISH.

There was other correspondence between Gov. Fish and Mr. Caldwell, and other parties, in relation to the best course to take to secure the property, which cannot now be found. From a memorandum in Mr. Caldwell's hand-writing, found among his papers, it is shown that on August 26, 1859, "a bundle" of letters were sent to a gentleman residing in Newburgh accompanied by a letter in which he says "I wish it understood that I do not wish my name brought forward prominently in your work, and not more than the history of the case requires."

ACTION BOARD SUPERVISORS OF ORANGE COUNTY.

On page 324, Proceedings of Board Supervisors on Thursday, Nov. 22, 1849, appears the following:

" Andrew J. Caldwell, Esq., appeared before the Board and stated that certain premises in Newburgh had been sold by the Loan Commissioners and bought in by them for the State; said premises are known by the name of Washington's Head Quarters. And also by request read a correspondence between himself and the Governor of the State on the subject of preserving the said premises for a public ground. And he also asked the co-operation of the Board in accomplishing that subject. On motion of Mr. Fullerton it was resolved that a Committee of three be appointed to take the subject in consideration, and report to the Board. Whereupon,

Daniel Fullerton, O. S. Hathaway and L. M. Ferris were appointed said Committee. It was on motion, Resolved that the Chairman of the Board be added to the Committee."

On page 335, Proceedings Board Supervisors, on Wednesday, Nov. 28th, of same year, is found as follows:

PETITION BOARD OF SUPERVISORS TO LEGISLATURE.

To the Legislature of the State of New York. The undersigned the Board of Supervisors of the County of Orange Respectfully represent:

That a portion of the monies deposited by the United States with the State of New York were loaned under the direction of the said State on security of certain premises known as Washington's Head Quarters, located in the village of Newburgh in the said County of Orange. And that on default of payment the said premises have been sold and bought in for and on behalf of the State.

That it is now the duty of the Loan Office of the said County under the existing law to dispose of said premises, and to restore the proceeds thereof to the fund from whence the same was derived.

That the stone building now standing on the said premises is on the Bank of the Hudson River in full view of the multitudes daily passing on its waters from all parts of the world and that it still remains unimpaired as when it was honored by the residence of Washington and LaFayette.

That the said mansion was the head-quarters of Washington for the last two years of the Revolutionary War, and was the last he occupied in the character of Commander-in-Chief, and was also the scene of his most glorious triumphs over the fearful designs of the celebrated "Newburgh Letters," and where he closed a military career unexampled in the history of the world.

That the people of Orange County could not witness without the deepest mortification the demolition or desecration of an edifice, endeared to them and to their fellow citizens

throughout the Union by so many Patriotic associations and
so intimately connected with the History of the Revolution.
While Forts Montgomery and Putnam, in its immediate
neighborhood, are mouldering in decay, your petitioners
desire that this venerable edifice may be spared, and every
possible exertion used to preserve and maintain it inviolate
under the ownership and protection of the Empire State.

Your Memorialists therefore in the name and in behalf of
the People of the County of Orange Respectfully pray that
your Honorable body will cause to be repaid to the United
States Deposit Fund the amount that appears from the last
annual report of the Commissioners of Loans of the County
of Orange to have been loaned upon the said premises and
retain the title of the same in the Government of this State,
and that you will further provide by necessary laws for its
preservation for all time to come,

And your petitioners will ever pray.

> DAVID H. MOFFATT, Chairman, Blooming Grove.
> DANIEL FULLERTON, Minisink.
> LINDLY MURRY FERRIS, Montgomery.
> WILLIAM V. B. ARMSTRONG, Warwick.
> ODELL S. HATHAWAY, Newburgh.
> A. P. THOMPSON, Mount Hope.
> DANIEL SWARTWOUT, Deerpark.
> R. M. VAIL, Goshen.
> WILLIAM JACKSON, Hamptonburgh.
> MORGAN SHUIT, Monroe.
> HEZEKIAH H. MOFFATT, Chester.
> JOHN DENNISTON, Cornwall.
> ABRAM VAIL, JR., Wallkill.
> AUGUSTUS THOMPSON, Crawford.

The towns are not appended to the names as they appear
on the record; they have been affixed by the author, to indi-
cate where they belonged. All are dead it is believed but
the Supervisor from Mt. Hope, A. P. Thompson, now
Cashier of the Port Jervis National Bank.

It will be noticed that there are but fourteen towns represented, J. R. Dickson, the Supervisor of the only other town in the county, not being present.

The Committee to whom the foregoing subject of Washington's Headquarters was referred, reported the foregoing petition, which was unanimously adopted and signed by all the members of the Board.

This memorial was written by Mr. Caldwell, as learned by a memorandum in his handwriting found among his papers, but was drawn up as a petition from the Supervisors to Congress, but subsequently changed and addressed to the Legislature.

From the subsequent action of the Governor it is gathered that the recommendation made by him to the Legislature was deemed by himself and Mr. Caldwell the best plan to take.

The following is an "extract from the Annual Message of Hon. Hamilton Fish, Governor of the State of New York, to the Legislature of 1850":

MESSAGE OF GOVERNOR FISH.

"The foreclosure of a mortgage, given to the Commissioners for loaning certain moneys of the United States, has vested in the State the title to a piece of land, and to the stone building, near Newburgh, in the County of Orange, known as 'Washington's Head-Quarters.' I respectfully submit that there are associations connected with this venerable edifice which rise above the consideration of dollars and cents, and which should distinguish it from other acquisitions and property of the State, and should prevent its being disposed of, unless for objects in some degree congenial with its past history. It is perhaps the last relic within the bounds of the State, and under the control of its Legislature, connected with the history of the illustrious man who left us this patriotic admonition."

[Here follows an extract from an address of George Washington:]

APPOINTMENT OF COMMITTEE.

Extract from the Assembly Journal, January 14, 1850.

*   *   *   *   *   *

Mr. Speaker announced the following select committees, to wit :   *   *   *   *   *   *

"On so much of the Annual Message of the Governor as relates to Washington's Head Quarters."

Mr. Leland, Mr. Truslow, Mr. Martin, Mr. Lyons, Mr. Lott.

[In Assembly March 6, 1850.]

Of the Select Committee in relation to the preservation of " Washington's Head Quarters."

REPORT OF ASSEMBLY COMMITTEE.

Mr. Leland, from the Select Committee, to which was referred so much of the Annual Message of the Governor as relates to Washington's Headquarters, and also the petition of the Board of Supervisors of Orange County, praying for an act causing to be repaid to the United States Deposit Fund the amount, that appears from the last annual report of the Commissioners of Loans of the County of Orange, to have been loaned upon the said premises and retain the title of the same in the government of the State ; and that we will further provide by necessary laws for its preservation for all time to come, having had the same under consideration,

REPORTS.

It is shown that the distinguished individuals whose names are appended to the petition submitted to the consideration of your Committee, are influenced by a laudable desire to preserve and perpetuate one of the most interesting monuments of the American Revolution.

Though the pages of history may transmit to posterity the events of that interesting period through all time : yet there are certain objects and places connected with our Revolutionary War which every American citizen delights to look upon, and around which he loves to call back the scenes that rendered them dear to his memory.

The chair in which John Hancock sat when he presided over the Convention of 1776, and when he affixed his name to the Declaration of American Independence, is now preserved with pious care, in the Capitol of Pennsylvania, where every intelligent and patriotic traveler visiting the city of Philadelphia fails not to examine that ancient remnant of Revolutionary times.

The old day-book in which Washington, in his own handwriting, kept his accounts during the Revolutionary War, is still preserved as a precious relic among our archives at the seat of our general government.

The citizens of our sister State of Massachusetts have made commendable efforts to preserve from desecration the ground on which was fought the battle of Bunker Hill. In contemplating such movements of our war of independence the best feelings of the heart are elicited and cherished.

If our love of country is excited when we read the biography of our revolutionary heroes, or the history of revolutionary events, how much more will the flame of patriotism burn in our bosoms when we tread the ground where was shed the blood of our fathers, or when we move among the scenes where were conceived and consummated their noble achievements. Let every true friend of our Country, with the liveliest fervor of heart, delight in the written pages of history, or the monuments of marble, or the ancient relics, or the memorable locality, or any other thing, which may transmit to our children a knowledge of the virtues of the fathers of the republic. It will be good for our citizens in these days of political collisions, in these days of political demagogueism: it will be good for them in these days when we hear the sound of disunion reiterated from every part of the Country; in all future time occasionally to chasten their minds by reviewing the history of our revolutionary struggle.

That the object of the petitioners may be more fully understood your Committee would state the following particulars: About fifty rods south of the village of Newburgh, in the County of Orange, there stands an ancient dwelling, built in an irregular form of rough stone, which was erected about one hundred years ago. It is now known in that vicinity by the name of the "Old Hasbrouck House," and in revolutionary times by the name of "Washington's Headquarters." It occupies a commanding eminence on the bank of the Hudson River overlooking the beautiful bay of Newburgh, and the military station at West Point, and taking within its range all the splendid water and mountain scenery for which that region is remarkable. In every direction from the house the eye may dwell upon views rich in natural beauty and historical recollections; West Point on the south, enthroned amidst the Highlands, was the scene of some of the most exciting incidents which characterized our revolutionary struggle; the beacon summits of Fishkill mountains, the camp-ground on Fishkill and Snake Hill plains, the location of the barracks, store-houses, and hospitals of our army, are all within a short distance from this interesting spot. The associations of the place call at once to the mind of every patriotic visitor many interesting occurrences connected with the names of Stuben, Kosciusko and Lafayette.

The "Hasbrouck House," which it is the design of the petitioners to perpetuate, was a long time the head-quarters of General Washington. It remains as yet in nearly the same condition as that in which Washington left it; but circumstances are such that it must soon fall unless efficient measures are taken to preserve it. It contains one room in the centre of the house which is about twenty-four feet square, but the ceiling is so low as to make it appear much larger. This room has seven doors and but one window; General Washington used it as his dining-room and parlor; at night it was converted into a bed-chamber for his staff officers and occasional visitors. On the north-east corner of the house, communicating with the large centre room, is a small chamber which General Washington used as a study or private office. Many revolutionary anecdotes have been told, the scenes of which were laid in the old square room at

Newburgh, with its seven doors and one window. When General Lafayette visited this country in 1824 he made a pilgrimage to this venerable mansion. After an absence of half a century his eyes could hardly be satisfied with examining the old rooms, and the little north-east room, the windows, the doors, the fire-place, the outside appearance, and the surrounding objects and scenery of that memorable place. But the most memorable affair connected with the subject remains to be mentioned. While the American army was encamped around the old "Hasbrouck House" near the close of the war there was conceived in their midst the most insidious and formidable treason that ever threatened the prosperity and honor of our Country. The war was about closing by the peace of 1783, with triumph and glory. The army was about to be discharged; they had endured the keenest privations; they had toiled and bled most nobly for their country, but had suffered for the want of clothing and provisions. Their pay had been withheld and Congress had manifested a reluctance from the embarrassed state of our finances, promptly to adjust their claims. Broken down with pecuniary embarrassment, and with hard service in the "tented field," our officers became discontented, and complained bitterly of the injustice of Congress, and the apparent ingratitude of their country. The prospect of an immediate disbandment in the midst of their poverty and suffering, without pay or even the adjustments of their accounts, was almost too much for even those noble-hearted men to endure. It was in the midst of this universal murmuring of discontent, on the 10th day of March, 1783, that the celebrated "Newburgh Letters" made their appearance. These letters were written in the most touching and powerful eloquence, and addressed to minds already chafed by disappointment and a sense of injustice. They pointed to a remedy for wrongs endured of a most desperate character; and had their counsel prevailed, our Revolutionary Army, at the very time of consummating the most glorious achievement the world ever witnessed, would have incurred indelible dishonor. It was in the small north-east room of this house

24 WASHINGTON'S HEADQUARTERS.

where Washington meditated upon these portentous letters and prepared himself to assuage the angry passions which were kindling with such fearful import throughout his army. Taking counsel of his own lofty mind, the imagination can almost conceive him, on that occasion as personating the genius of American liberty, dictating his orders for a general meeting of his officers, and preparing an address containing arguments and appeals which fastened upon the very souls of his auditors, brought them unanimously to confide in the justice of their country, and hushed their rising passions forever. In the eloquent language in which Washington closed his address, our army, "gave one more distinguished proof of unexampled patriotism and patient virtue, rising superior to the pressure of the most complicated suffering," and by the dignity of their conduct have afforded "occasion for posterity to say, when speaking of the glorious example they have exhibited to mankind, had that day been wanting, the world had never seen the last stage of perfection, to which human nature is capable of attaining." It was but a few days after this event that Washington disbanded a portion of his army on the lawn before the door of this antiquated house. The hardy soldiers, whose hearts never quailed under danger or toil, melted into tears as they bade each other a lasting farewell on the consecrated ground which the petitioners seek to commemorate.

The Committee believe that the object which the petitioners have in view—"to preserve and perpetuate Washington's headquarters, in the village of Newburgh"—is worthy of their high character, and eminently deserving of legislative sanction. No traveler who touches upon the shores of Orange county will hesitate to make a pilgrimage to this beautiful spot, associated as it is with so many delightful reminiscences in our early history, and if he have an American heart in his bosom, he will feel himself a better man; his patriotism will kindle with deeper emotion; his aspirations of his country's good will ascend from a more devout mind for having visited the "HEAD QUARTERS OF WASHINGTON."

INTRODUCTION OF A BILL IN LEGISLATURE TO BUY THE HEAD QUARTERS.

In answer to the prayer of the petitioners the Committee ask leave to introduce a bill.   *   *   *

The bill was passed by a unanimous vote and became a law by signature of the Governor, April 10, 1850, becoming Chapter 265 of the laws of that year. This bill appropriated $2,391.02, and authorized the Commissioners of the Land Office to purchase certain premises known as Washington's Head quarters," the amount to be paid to the Commissioners of Loans of Orange county. It also appropriated $6,000 to purchase other lots and parcels of ground formerly attached to and part of Washington's Head-quarters. As at the time of the original purchase the house stood quite near to the south line of the lot, the Trustees appointed by the act saw that upon the adjoining property at some time in the future, buildings might be erected whose character would be detrimental to the property which they had in charge, so they secured the passage of an act by the Legislature appropriating $5,000 to buy a strip of land along the whole south side, thus receding the line further from the house. This rounded up and completed the work INITIATED by Mr. Caldwell. The State came into possession absolutely and forever, and private parties who wanted to make a gigantic speculation out of the old historic spot were foiled in their purpose. The original act appointing Trustee, also provided for a succession, and an annual appropriation is made to pay the " Keeper's " salary, who in addition has his rent free and any gratuity he may receive from visitors, though no CHARGE is made or asked from visitors.

Thus was this spot, which has become the shrine of the lovers of Liberty the world over and the Mecca of all those

WASHINGTON'S HEAD-QUARTERS. NEWBURGH

who reverence true greatness, rescued and preserved for all time.

That which has been presented above it is believed was unknown history. It certainly has been unwritten history, and has the merit of truthfulness, and has been written with a purpose—to give honor where and to whom honor is ue, and as a memorial to a revered father [who, as a compatriot and college mate of the immortal Robert Emmet, in his youth feeling the iron heel of despotism in his native land, Ireland, was with all his father's numerous family " sent out of the land in haste" by the order of a tyranical government choosing with them the United States as " The Land of Promise" and adoption] took every occasion afterward to instill into the minds of all his children the loftiest principles of patriotism, pointing especially to the example and conduct of Washington under the temptation of the " Newburgh Letters."

In 1824 Lafayette made his fourth and last visit to the United States, taking an extended tour throughout the whole country. He was greatly delighted at the evidences which he everywhere saw of its prosperity, and rejoiced in the stalwart growth of the young Republic, whose entrance (a half century previous) into the family of nations he had so

---

Since the dedication of the Headquarters which occurred July 4, 1850, 250.000 persons have registered their names on the books kept there for that purpose; this does not include residents of Newburgh, and these visitors have been of every color, nationality, and degree of social position from the plebeian to the titled man and woman, all coming reverently to worship at this Shrine of Liberty. To show the gradual increase of this visitation the number for 1851 (the first full year) and the numbers for the last several years are given : 1851, 4,624.

For 1880,					14,361
" 1881,	-	-	-	-	19,962
" 1882,		-	-	-	19,471
" 1883,	-	-	-	-	22,835
" 1884,		-	-	-	20,148
" 1885,	-	-	-	-	20,534
" 1886,		-	-	-	22,568

139,889

THE ROOM WITH SEVEN DOORS AND ONE WINDOW.

efficiently aided. He came to Newburgh to again revisit the place where such important events had transpired in which he had been so conspicuous an actor. His own Head Quarters in that early period were about two miles south of "The Old Hasbrouck House," on the "Vale of Avoca," near what is now known as Quassaic Creek. Visiting in 1824 the old house at Newburgh, and entering it, it was some time before the old man could "find his bearing." Going around the room touching here and there some part of the compartment, he at last exclaimed, "It is! it is! the very same, the room with seven doors and one window," now known as such the world over.

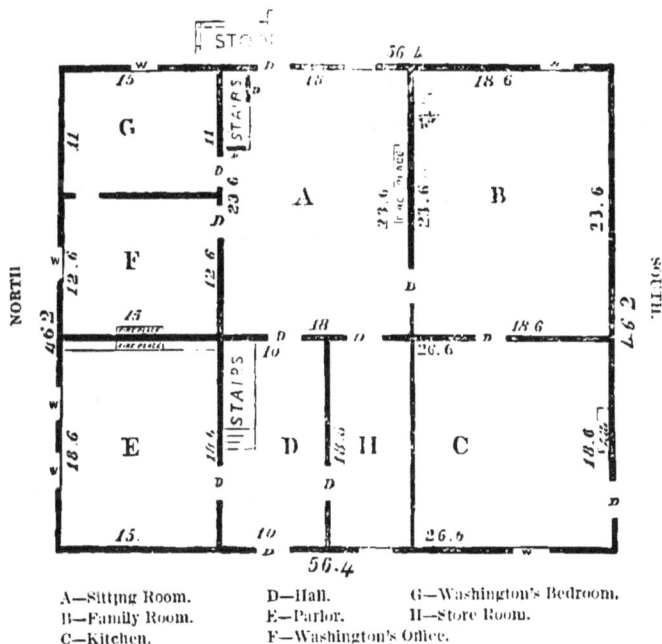

A—Sitting Room.   D—Hall.   G—Washington's Bedroom.
B—Family Room.   E—Parlor.   H—Store Room.
C—Kitchen.   F—Washington's Office.

DIAGRAM OF THE INTERIOR OF THE FIRST STORY OF WASHINGTON'S HEADQUARTERS.

It is but just to Mr. Campbell to say that though not so prominent in the transaction as his associate Loan Commissioner, Mr. Caldwell, he was in entire sympathy and accord with the latter in all his efforts to secure to the State a permanent title to the Head Quarters property. Alexander Campbell, who belonged to the Society of Friends, was born in Argyleshire, Scotland, Nov. 26, 1793, and emigrated to the United States in September, 1806. The likeness of him given was taken when he was sixty years of age. He was respected for his kindness of heart, which indeed expressed itself on his countenance.

PROMINENT EVENTS CONNECTED WITH THE NEWBURGH HEADQUARTERS.

It is believed that it will be most appropriate, as the history of the acquisition of this historic spot has been given, to refer to the event which more than any other connected with it, makes it pre-eminently historic, and to all lovers of our beloved land, the event of all others, and Washington's connected therewith, which has added the crowning luster to his name.

On the 3d day of September, 1783, at Paris, the treaty of peace between Great Britain and the United States was signed by the respective representatives of each government. On the 18th day of October Congress issued an order that on the 3d day of November the army which had through the long seven years' conflict maintained the struggle should be disbanded. The preliminaries of peace, however, had been signed on the 20th of January previous. The army seeing that disbandment must before long ensue, and that Congress had not made, and did not appear to be making any efforts to provide for their long arrearages of pay, or to even to adjust their accounts, became restive, and ready to listen to the suggestions of evil-minded persons. On the 11th of March, 1783, there appeared an "address to the army," with no name attached. This "address" was composed with great ingenuity, and calculated to inflame the rising passions of the army. The following extract is given:

["History of the War of the Independence of the United States of America," by Charles Botta.]

"After a pursuit of seven years the object for which we set out is at length brought within our reach. Yes, my friends, that suffering courage was active once; it has conducted the United States of America through a doubtful and bloody war. It has placed her in the chair of independency, and peace returns again to bless. Whom? A country willing to redress your wrongs, cherish your worth and reward your services? A country courting your return to private life, with tears of gratitude and smiles of admiration, longing to divide with you those riches which your wounds have preserved. Is this the case? or is it rather a country that tramples upon your rights, disdains your cries, and insults your distresses? Have you not more than once suggested your wishes, and made known your wants to Congress, wants and wishes which gratitude and policy should have anticipated, rather than evaded. And have you not lately, in the meek language of entreating memorials, begged from their justice what you could no longer expect from their favor? Have you been answered? Let the letter of your delegates to Philadelphia reply. If this then be your treatment while the swords you wear are necessary for the defense of America, what have you to expect when your voice shall sink and your strength dissipate by division, when those swords, the instruments and companions of your glory, shall be taken from your sides, and no remaining mark of military distinction left, but your wants, informities and scars? Can you then consent to be the only sufferers by this revolution, and retiring from the field grow old in poverty, wretchedness and contempt? Can you consent to wade through the mire of dependency and owe the miserable remnants of that life to charity, which has hitherto been spent in honor? If you can, go; and carry with you the jest of Tories and the scorn of Whigs; the ridicule, and, what is worse, the pity of the world. Go; starve and be forgotten! But if your spirit should revolt at this; if you have sense enough to discover, and spirit enough to oppose tyranny, under whatever garb it may assume, whether it be the plain coat of republicanism or the splendid robe of royalty; if you have yet learned to discriminate between a people and a CAUSE, between men and principles, awake; attend to your situation and REDRESS YOURSELVES. If the PRESENT MOMENT be lost, every future effort is vain; and your threats will be as empty as your entreaties now."

The effect was to "chafe minds already exasperated into a delirium of fury."

WASHINGTON'S ACTION.

Washington saw the rising storm, and determined to turn aside its violence. He issued orders calling upon his general and field officers, and one officer from each company in the army, to assemble, that they might deliberate upon the measures to be adopted for obtaining the redress of their grievances.

WASHINGTON'S GENERAL ORDER CALLING FOR A MEETING OF HIS OFFICERS.

HEAD QUARTERS, NEWBURGH, March 11, 1783.

The Commander-in-Chief having heard that a general meeting of the officers of the army was to be held this day at the New Building, in an anonymous letter which was circulated yesterday by some unknown person, conceives (although he is fully persuaded that the good sense of the officers would induce them to pay very little attention to such an irregular invitation) his duty as well as the true interests of the army requires his disapprobation of such disorderly proceedings, at the same time he requests the General and Field officers, with one officer from the Staff of the army, will assemble at 12 o'clock on Saturday next, at the New Building, to hear the report of the Committee of the Army to Congress. After mature deliberation they will advise what further measures ought to be adopted as most rational and best calculated to attain the just and important object in view. The senior officer in rank present will be pleased to preside and report the result of the deliberations to the Commander-in-Chief.

On the next day, after the issuance of this order by Washington, a second anonymous letter appeared to the effect that they must act with energy in the assembly which was to meet on the 15th of March, at the "Temple," or "New Building," a large log building which had been erected for the purpose of Sunday worship and other meetings, situate about three miles south-west from the Head Quarters. In the meantime Washington was not idle. He called into his counsel those tried and trusty patriots—Knox, Steuben, Putnam, Green. Wayne and others, each name the impersonation of loyalty. And in the little north-east room they met and approved of his purpose to attend the meeting and address the malcontents. In conversation with others he appealed to the patriotism of some, he reminded others of the exhausted condition of the public treasury, and that he himself had not received one cent of pay from the beginning of the war, and on others he brought to bear other motives and and appeals.

The meeting was held and fully attended. It was a grave occasion. When the assembly had been called to order by General Gates, Washington stepped forward and delivered the well-known masterly written address, which chained their attention, in language clear and compact, mild

yet severe, elevated and dignified, and withal so loyal to
patriotic principles, that the whole mutinous scheme was
overthrown in the deliberative conference which followed.
More than forty years transpired before it was ascertained
that the author of the incendiary address was Major John
Armstrong, an aid to Gen. Gates. [From "Washington's
orders issued at Newburgh," compiled by Major Edward C.
Boynton, of Newburgh, one of the Trustees Washington's
Headquarters.]

Assembled with his officers and men in the Temple he
took from his pocket his "address," and putting on his
spectacles he said, "These eyes, my friends, have grown
dim, and these locks white in the service, yet I never
doubted the justice of my country."

EXTRACT FROM THE "ADDRESS."

"My God!" he exclaimed, "what can this writer have in
view by recommending such measures? Can he be a friend
to the army? Can he be a friend to this country? Rather
is he not an insidious foe; some emissary from NEW YORK,
plotting the ruin of both by sowing the seed of discord and
separation between the civil and military authorities of the
continent? Let me entreat you, gentlemen, not to take any
measures which, viewed in the calm light of reason, will
lessen the dignity and sully the glory you have hitherto
maintained; let me request you to rely on the plighted faith
of your country, and place full confidence in the purity of
the intentions of Congress, that previous to your dissolution
as an army, they will cause all your accounts to be fairly
liquidated, and that they will adopt the most effectual
measures in their power to render ample justice to you for
your faithful and meritorious services. And let me conjure
you in the name of our common country, as you value your
own sacred honor, as you respect the rights of humanity, and
as you regard the military and national honor of America,
to express the utmost horror and detestation of the man who

wishes under any specious pretenses to overthrow the liberties of our country; and who wickedly attempts to open the flood gates of civil discord, and deluge our rising empire with blood."

"By thus determining, and thus acting, you will pursue the plain and direct road to the attainment of your wishes; you will defeat the insidious designs of our enemies who are compelled to resort from open force to secret artifice."

It will appear from the above partial extracts that while the appeal in the Armstrong letters was most artfully conceived, with a purpose to inflame the minds of officers and men, the "address" of Washington, evolved in his mind and written in the little north-east room of "The Old Stone House," was equally adroit in appealing to their patriotism, their sense that justice to them would be done by Congress, and that it was a SECRET ENEMY who was thus endeavoring to accomplish in this way what arms had failed to do.

CONJECTURES.

Fancy attempts in vain to picture that 15th day of March, 1783, when Washington with his assembled officers about him, stood in the "Temple." Was it a bleak, cold March day—"winter lingering in the lap of Spring?" Did the east wind drive before it over the "Beacon" heights dark, forbidding storm clouds, emblematical of the black cloud of sedition gathering in the breasts of those desperate soldiers? Or was it one of those rare Spring days which sometimes surprise us even in March, when throughout the great "Gate of the Highlands" soft winds came laden with promise of coming beauty, and bird songs here and there are harbingers of hope? Did Washington, as he looked down between the portals of "Storm King" and "Break Neck," toward the plains of West Point turn in thought to that other previous dark day in the history of the young Republic? Did he remember how that damnable treason of Arnold was discovered and thwarted by the watchful patriotism of John Paulding, David Williams and Isaac Van Wert, and did he take refuge in the hope that the same watchful Providence which had averted the former disaster, would guard our country in its present danger?

What his thoughts were we cannot know. In that moment of extreme peril he was as always, the strong, self-poised, imperturbable man, hopeful for his country.

"There is but one straight course, and that is to seek truth, and to pursue it steadily."   WASHINGTON.

Thus Washington stilled the rising waters of sedition among his officers and soldiers, and dashed from his own lips the tempting, though poisoned chalice which concealed in its contents a THRONE, and thereby most worthily imitated the conduct of his Divine Exemplar, who, "on an exceeding high mountain," nearly eighteen centuries before, met the offer of, "All these things will I give thee" with "Get thee hence satan." "There is no doubt that had Washington so desired he could at this time have founded a Monarchy, sustained by the bayonets of his army. He took the course on the contrary, of quelling this disposition on the part of his soldiers wherever it showed itself."

"He was a man, take him for all in all,
We ne'er shall look upon his like again."—SHAKESPEARE.

There are four events in the history of the Revolutionary struggle which are intimately connected with the Head Quarters locality. First, the refusal of Washington on May 22, 1782, to accept a crown offered to him in an address presented by Colonel Nicola. He met this proposal in these ever memorable words : " I am much at a loss to conceive what part of my conduct could have given encouragement to an address which to me seems big with the greatest mischiefs which can befall my country. Let me conjure you then, if you have any regard for your country, concern for yourselves, or posterity, or respect for me, to banish these thoughts from your mind, and never communicate as from yourself or any one else a sentiment of a like nature." The second event was the suppression of a movement to seize upon the government, already narrated ; the third the proclamation of the cessation of hostilities with the Mother Country, and the fourth the disbandment of the army, Nov. 3, 1783.

In view of the fact that the State is in possession of the property ; that Newburgh is in the enjoyment of that possession, though neither knowing of the men and means by whom and which that possession and enjoyment were secured, the following is not inapplicable :

My name and my place and my tomb all forgotten ;
The brief race of time, well and patiently run ;
So let me pass away, peacefully, silently ;
Only remembered by what I have done.

I need not be missed, if another succeed me,
To reap down those fields which in spring-time I've sown ;
He who plowed and who sowed, is not missed by the reaper ;
He is only remembered by what he has done.

So let my living be, so be my dying ;
So let my name lie unblazoned, unknown,
Unpraised and unmissed ; I shall still be remembered ;
Yes ! but remembered by what I have done.

On the 4th day of July, 1850, the property which had been preserved from the grasp of private speculation, and in the manner foretold, secured in possession of the State forever, was dedicated. From the very meagre account which is found in the Newburgh Gazette of July 10, 1850, the following extract is given; and it is an instance of the progress of journalism from that day to this that an event of such interest at the time did not call out more journalistic enterprise in giving a fuller report than the one the Gazette did, so different from the exceedingly interesting and exhaustive account that the Newburgh Journal gave of the subsequent Centennial celebration, held on the same grounds. The Gazette says "that by noon 10,000 strangers were in town, Gen. Winfield Scott came from West Point, and hundreds called on him at the United States Hotel. A street procession followed; arrived at the Head Quarters; after singing an Ode written by Mrs. Mary E. Monell, the flag was raised by Gen. Scott. He then addressed the crowd, and after him John W. Edmonds "—(Judge Edmonds of the Supreme Court, residing at Poughkeepsie)—" the orator of the day, then Frederick J. Betts, John J. Monell and William F. Fullerton."

The following is taken from the Gazette July 10, 1850.

ODE SUNG AT THE DEDICATION OF THE OLD BUILDING JULY 4TH, 1850.

Composed by Mary E. Monell.

Freeman pause! this ground is holy;
  Noble spirits suffered here;
Tardy justice marching slowly,
    Tried their faith from year to year;
      Yet their patience
Conquered every doubt and fear.

Sacred is this mansion hoary !
  Neath its roof-tree years ago,
Dwelt the father of our glory,
  He whose name appalled the foe :
    Greater honor
    Home nor hearth can never know.

Unto him and them are owing,
  Peace as stable as our hills :
Plenty like yon river flowing,
  To the sea from thousand rills :
    Love of country,
    Love that every bosom thrills.

Brothers! to your care is given,
  Safe to keep this hallowed spot ;
Though our warriors rest in heaven,
  And their places know them not,
    See ye to it
    That their deeds be ne'er forget.

With a prayer your faith expressing,
  Raise your country's flag on high :
Here where rests a nation's blessing,
  Stars and stripes shall float for aye :
    Mutely telling
    Stirring tales of days gone by.

Since the foregoing, in manuscript, was placed in the
hands of the publishers, with great delight the following
letter from the Hon. Hamilton Fish, the prominent public
actor in the history just given, has been received by the
author. It explains itself, and supplies the "missing link"
in the transaction. The venerable writer is now in his
seventy-ninth year of age, and judging from the hand-
writing of the letter, as the public will on reading the subject matter, "his eye is not dim nor his natural force abated."

NEW YORK, Jan. 24, 1887.

RICHARD CALDWELL, ESQ., Middletown, Orange Co., N. Y.

DEAR SIR:—Your letter of the 22d inst. was duly received. I am pleased to learn from it that a true account of
what led to the securing to the State of New York the

possession of the Washington's Head Quarters near
Newburgh is to be prepared, and that you have undertaken
its preparation.

I have a vivid recollection of the incident. Mr. Andrew
J. Caldwell (your father) was one of the Commissioners for
loaning the U. S. Deposit Fund (as it was called) in Orange
County, and in his discharge of the duties of his office, on
the default of payment on a mortgage on the property
known as the "Old Hasbrouck House," (Washington's
Quarters) foreclosed their mortgage, and advised me, being
then Governor of the State, of the facts, and suggested the
importance of its preservation to the State, as an important
and valuable memorial of past associations. The idea im-
pressed me most favorably, and I determined to lose no
opportunity to carry out his patriotic and large-minded sug-
gestion. The idea of preserving this property to the State
originated with Mr. Caldwell. In addition to the letters,
of which you send me copies, namely, one from Mr. Caldwell to
me, dated Salisbury Mills, Oct. 1, 1849, and my reply,
dated New York, Oct. 6, 1849, I find only one letter from
Mr. Caldwell, dated Salisbury Mills, 28th of October, 1849,
in which he says: "Though the intelligent and public-spirited
portion of that community (the village of Newburgh) are
warmly in favor of the object proposed, no public expression of their views and wishes has yet taken place. The
subject, however, has been taken up in a more influential
quarter, and one not liable to suspicion of local or interested
motives. The Board of Supervisors, the local Legislature
of the county, have had their attention directed to the subject, and have passed resolutions and prepared a memorial
to the Legislature, praying that provision be made for pro-
tecting and improving the premises, as public property, and
preserving the "Old Stone House," in its original form and
construction. It is also proposed that application be made
to Congress to release and remit to the State of New York
that portion of the United States Deposit Fund which was
loaned on the premises aforesaid, on such conditions and
with such guarantees as may best secure the preservation

and improvement of the same, to be held by the State as a public ground, inalienable forever." The letter then proceeded to state that "the Board of Supervisors meet again to-day. I am promised a copy of their Resolutions and Memorial, and if they appear worthy of your attention, may take the liberty to forward them."

Acknowledging this letter, 30th Oct., (the day of its reception) I wrote Mr. Caldwell that I had made the subject "a matter of reference in my message, which has been in print for some days." The message had been submitted confidentially to the consideration and advice of the State officers, (as it was the cabinet of the Governor) and the particular passage referring to the Head Quarters had been most cordially approved. I did not favor the idea of applying to Congress for any aid in the matter, thinking it beneath the dignity of the State of New York to accept, much less to ask assistance, for such an object from any quarter. I aided and advised in the preparation of the bill, which passed the Legislature, and exercised what influence I could exercise to secure its enactment. But the subject met with such favor that there was but little difficulty in the adoption of the law. The State made good the amount to the United States Deposit Fund. You have the act as it was passed and the copy of the Governor's message of Jan. 1st, 1850, and I need not refer to them. I do not find any other correspondence between Mr. A. J. Caldwell and myself than the four letters to which I have referred. I hope that your publication may prove a substantial pecuniary benefit to the benevolent association to which you generously propose to appropriate its proceeds. If you think proper to insert a likeness of myself in the book I enclose a photograph as you request taken some years since, but several years after I had ceased to hold the office of Governor; in fact photographing at that time was, if known at all, in its infancy. With much respect,

I am, my dear sir, very truly yours,

HAMILTON FISH.

As a part of the history connected with the Head
Quarters, the following facts in the life of Washington, and
those sterling patriots whom he gathered about him during
the nearly two years of his army life at Newburgh are given:

WASHINGTON, COMMANDER-IN-CHIEF OF THE ARMY OF THE REVOLUTION.

Born in Westmorland County, Va., Feb. 22, 1732.

Died at Mount Vernon, Va., Dec. 14, 1799.

Married Mrs. Martha Custis when he was 15 years of age,
Jan 17, 1759.

Elected Commander-in-Chief by the Continental Congress
while he was a Member of the Virginia Assembly, May 10,
1775, being then 43 years old.

Took command at Cambridge, July 2, 1875.

Nov. 2, 1783, issued at Princeton, N. J., his farewell address to the army of the United States.

Resigned his commission at Annapolis, Md., Dec. 19, 1783,
Returned to Mount Vernon, Dec. 23, 1783.

Chosen first President and inaugurated at New York,
April 30, 1789.

Refused third election and issued his "farewell address to
the country" 1796.

Was a member of the Church of England.

Was six feet two inches high, brown hair, blue eyes, large
head and frame, weighing 209 pounds.

By Washington's will, dated Feb. 9, 1799, he manumitted
all his slaves, 124 in number. The will is long, and George
Washington's name is written at the bottom of every page.

"First in war, first in peace, first in the hearts of
his countrymen."

MAJOR GEN. LAFAYETTE.

Marie Jean Paul Roch Yves Gilbert Martien Marques D. Lafayette.

Born Sept. 6, 1757, in Castle of Chavagnac Dept., Loire, France. Died May 20, 1834. In 1777 he came to America to take part in the War of the Revolution. Not at first receiving the rank and commission that had been promised him before leaving France he wrote to Congress thus: "After the sacrifice I have made I have the right to exact two favors—one is to serve at my own expense, the other to serve at first as a volunteer." In 1784, after the close of the war, he made his third visit to the United States; visited Washington at Mount Vernon, and everywhere was received with unbounded enthusiasm.

In 1824 he visited America for the last time; laid the corner stone of Bunker Hill Monument, and on Sept. 8, embarked on the government war ship Brandywine, especially detailed to convey him to France. It was during this trip "that he visited Congress, and was received by that body with distinguished honor. It voted $140,000 as payment in part for the money he had expended on our behalf. He had clothed and fed our naked, starving soldiers at his own cost, expended money for the State, fought our battles, endured, suffered, and toiled for our welfare; yet he never asked, never expected compensation. It had been entirely a free-will offering—his youth, his wealth, his life, all, an unselfish, noble sacrifice to to a weak but brave people, struggling to be free." [Washington and His Generals.—Headley.]

MAJOR-GENERAL NATHANIEL GREEN.

Born in Warwick, R. I., May 27, 1742. Died June 19, 1786. Member Rhode Island Legislature 1770. When the

war broke out he joined the army, and by the Society of
Friends, of which he was a member, was expelled.   Made
Brigadier-General June 22, 1775, and Major-General Aug. 9,
1776.   President of Court Martial on Major Andre's trial.
Took command of the army of the South, at Charleston,
Dec. 2, 1780.   Congress voted him a gold medal, commem-
orative of the battle of Eutaw Springs.   Considered the
ablest general in the army next to Washington.

MAJOR-GENERAL PUTNAM.

Born in Salem, Mass., Jan. 17, 1718.   Died in Brooklyn,
Conn., May 29, 1790.   Member of Connecticut Legislature.
In 1777 he was in command in the Highlands, N., Y., and
with far-seeing wisdom selected West Point on the Hudson
as the site of a fortress.   In 1778 took his perilous break-
neck ride down the side of a precipice at West Greenwich,
Conn, escaping from those who thought his capture secured.
While in command in the Highlands, a Tory spy was captured, tried and sentenced to death.   Sir Henry Clinton, in
command at New York, sent a flag of truce to Gen. Putnam,
demanding the release of the man, to which the General
replied :

" HEAD QUARTERS, 7th Aug., 1777.
" Edward Palmer, an officer in the enemy's service, was
taken as a spy, lurking within our lines, he has been tried as a
spy, condemned as a spy, and shall be executed as a spy, and
the flag is ordered to depart immediately.

"ISRAEL PUTNAM."
" P. S.—He has been executed accordingly."

MAJOR-GENERAL ANTHONY WAYNE.

Called " Mad Anthony Wayne " from his impetuosity and
the fierceness of his charges.   Born in Chester County, Pa.,

Jan. 1, 1745. Died on Presque Isle, 15th Dec., 1796. Farmer and land surveyor until 1774. Member Pennsylvania Legislature 1774-1775. Raised regiment Sept. 17, 1775. Made a Colonel January 1, 1776, Brigadier-General Feb. 21, 1777. Captured Stony Point at night July 15, 1779, for which Congress gave him a vote of thanks and a gold medal. When asked by General Washington if he could storm the fort he replied, " General, if you will only plan it, I will storm the infernal regions."

MAJOR-GENERAL STEUBEN.

Born in Prussia. Died Nov. 28, 1797. Aid-de-Camp to King of Prussia. Arrived in the United States Dec. 1777. Entered the army as volunteer, on the condition if his services were not satisfactory or the United States not successful, he was not to receive pay. " We are beginning to walk," he said after the storming and capture of Stony Point. One of Court Martial to try Andre.

MAJOR-GENERAL KNOX.

Born in Boston, July 25th, 1750. Died in Thomaston, Me., Oct. 27, 1800. Aid to General Ward at Bunker Hill. Sent to Canada to bring artillery across the country, and as a reward for his success was placed in command over the artillery. On Court Martial which tried Andre. One of the Commissioners to arrange the terms of peace after the close of the war. Secretary of War under Washington, and for eleven years.

First proposed "The Society of the Cincinnatti." Death caused by swallowing a chicken bone. Weighed 280 pounds.

ACKNOWLEDGEMENTS.

The author desires thankfully to place on record his indebtedness to Secretary of State, Frederick Cook, of Albany, N. Y., for extracts from public papers in the State archives, the manuscript of which will be preserved by him as most beautiful specimens of penmanship. Also to D. C. Contant, City Clerk of Newburgh, for transcripts from old village records, and for courtesies received from the Clerk of the Board of Supervisors of Orange County in giving access to old records; to the Hon. Hamilton Fish and the representatives of Alexander Campbell for photographs respectively loaned, from which plates were taken; to the Newburgh Journal for plates loaned, and last, but by no means least, to the Middletown Press, for very liberal terms of publication, resulting as it is hoped it will, through the liberality of a generous public, in a large resultant benefit to "The Ladies' Home Society of Orange County."

Do you read the PRESS? You should if you do not. The Semi-Weekly edition issued Tuesdays and Fridays, $2.00 per year; $1.00 for six months; 50 cents for three months. Sample copies free.

The Daily Edition 50 cents per month. Postpaid to any address.

If you want any printing done, such as Books, Pamphlets, Posters, Bill and Letter Heads, Invitations, Programmes. Envelopes, Price Lists, Circulars, or any work in the printing line, send to the PRESS Office for samples and prices.

STIVERS, SLAUSON & BOYD,
Middletown, N. Y.

A TRUE HISTORY

OF

THE ACQUISITION

OF

WASHINGTON'S HEADQUARTERS

AT NEWBURGH,

BY THE STATE OF NEW YORK.

BY RICHARD CALDWELL,

SALISBURY MILLS, N. Y.

PEASE'S
HONEY, HOREHOUND,

HEALTH IS BETTER THAN RICHES.

LICORICE AND TAR

HAS ABSOLUTELY NO EQUAL FOR THE CURE OF

COUGHS COLDS, BRONCHITIS,

Croupy Tendencies, Difficult Breathing, and all affections of the Throat and Lungs, *making rapid and permanent cures*, and thereby preventing Consumption.

Pease's Honey, Horehound, Licorice and Tar

Is a remarkably efficacious remedy, and contains nothing whatever injurious to the most delicate constitution. It soothes and allays all irritation and inflammation, giving strength and tone to the tissues, enabling them to endure the atmospheric changes.

This celebrated remedy is prepared by the Grandson of **John Pease,** the originator of Horehound Candy, and has no equal. No one's stock is complete without it, and every family should have it in their home.

☞*Beware of weak and worthless Imitations similar in name.*

Ask for **Pease's Honey, Horehound, Licorice and Tar.** Buy and receive healing. **Take no Substitute.**

Three sizes : 25c., 50c., and $1.00. The 50c. size is a Pocket Flask and very convenient for gentlemen. The two larger sizes are cheaper in proportion

CHAS. G. PEASE, Prop., New York.

Trade Supplied by **THURBER, WHYLAND & CO.**

www.ingramcontent.com/pod-product-compliance
Lightning Source LLC
Chambersburg PA
CBHW021644270326
41931CB00008B/1156